THE LITTLE WORLD OF
HUMONGO BONGO

ChiGraphic

FIRST EDITION

The Little World of Humongo Bongo © 2018 by George A. Romero
Cover design © 2018 by Erik Mohr
Cover flat and interior design © 2018 by Samantha Beiko & Jared Shapiro
Illustrations © 2018 by George A. Romero
Foreword © 2018 by Tony Timpone
Interview © 2018 by Dave Alexander

Library and Archives Canada Cataloguing in Publication

Romero, George A.
[Petit monde d'Humongo Dongo. English]
    The little world of Humongo Bongo / [written and illustrated by]
    George A. Romero

Translation of: Le petit monde d'Humongo Dongo.
Issued in print and electronic formats.
ISBN 978-1-77148-443-5 (softcover).--ISBN 978-1-77148-444-2 (PDF)

    I. Title. II. Title: Humongo Bongo. III. Title: Petit monde
d'Humongo Dongo. English

PZ7.R67Lit 2017   j813'.54   C2017-904472-9
                                           C2017-904473-7

CHIZINE PUBLICATIONS
Peterborough, Canada
www.chizinepub.com
info@chizinepub.com

Copyedited by Sandra Kasturi
Proofread by Brett Savory

Distributed in Canada by
Fitzhenry & Whiteside Limited
195 Allstate Parkway
Markham, Ontario L3R 4T8
Telephone: (905) 477-9700
e-mail: bookinfo@fitzhenry.ca

Distributed in the U.S. by
Consortium Book Sales & Distribution
34 Thirteenth Avenue, NE, Suite 101
Minneapolis, MN 55413
Phone: (612) 746-2600
e-mail: sales.orders@cbsd.com

We acknowledge the support of the Canada Council for the Arts which last year invested $20.1 million in writing and publishing throughout Canada.

ONTARIO ARTS COUNCIL
CONSEIL DES ARTS DE L'ONTARIO

an Ontario government agency
un organisme du gouvernement de l'Ontario

Published with the generous assistance of the Ontario Arts Council.

Printed in Canada

THE LITTLE WORLD OF
HUMONGO BONGO

FOREWORD BY TONY TIMPONE

GEORGE A. ROMERO

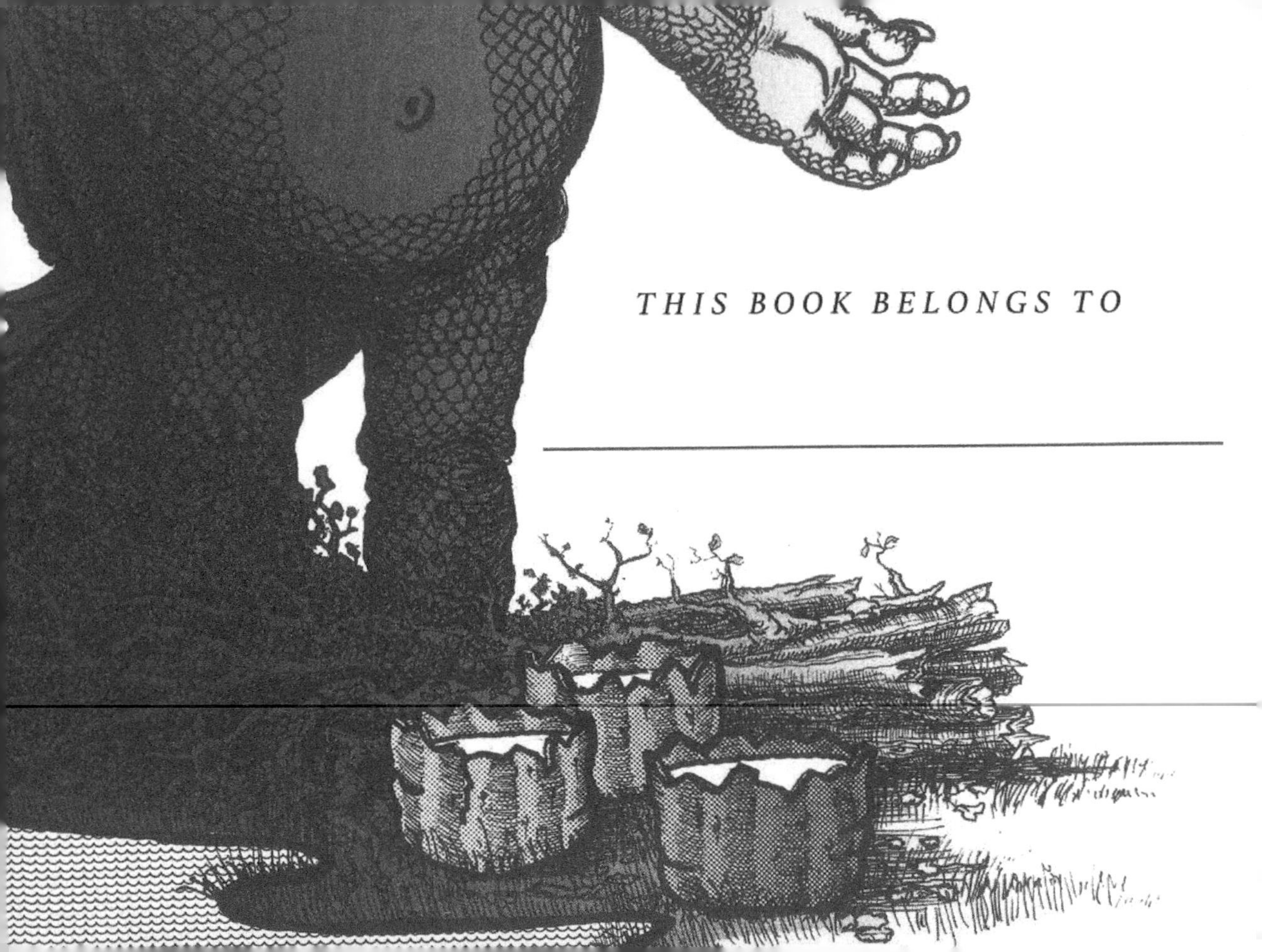

THIS BOOK BELONGS TO

To Tina and Suzanne with love.

FOREWORD

George A. Romero: A Kid at Heart

The last person you would expect to find writing a children's book would be George A. Romero, right? The man who invented the modern zombie film? The auteur who introduced graphic gore to the malls of America? The independent film trailblazer who inspired a generation of future horror hounds? But those who knew him best, or even knew him casually, can tell you that George's introduction as a modern Dr. Seuss is long overdue.

I first met George at a horror convention in 1978. I was just a 15-year-old kid. He was a 38-year-old 6-foot 4-inch *kid*, gleefully mingling and greeting the fans who had gathered to see a stage presentation teasing his latest film, *Dawn of the Dead*, the long-awaited sequel to his B&W classic *Night of the Living Dead*. That first movie of George's celebrates its 50th anniversary this year. And 2018 also marks the debut of the English-language version of George's *The Little World of Humongo Bongo*, the children's book you now hold in your mitts, one destined to charm kids of all ages.

In *The Little World of Humongo Bongo*, George creates a wonderfully whimsical world. I question the use of *Little* in the title, as there is nothing little about it when the hero of the story, the 98-year-old scaly giant Bongo, stands taller than the highest treetop. With simple but evocative prose, George describes the unique realm of a planet called Tongo, where the rivers run with milk, where melons are as big as elephants. Three moons, streaking meteors, and thousands of stars fill the night sky. The child-like Bongo is a conflicted, peace-loving being, whose opinions of life get turned topsy-turvy when he meets a Lilliputian-esque race of humanoids, called the Peanut people.

But like the best of George's movies, which he infused with intelligent and sometimes scathing social commentary, you can find many metaphors and concerns for the future of our own species threaded through George's words. A well-known liberal, George has something to say in *The Little World of Humongo Bongo* about intolerance, overpopulation, the environment, and even our notion of God. Fortunately, as in all of George's fantasies, none of this is heavy-handed. His main goal here is to tell a fun, page-turning fantasy fable, the kind he read to his own children when they were young. And that you can now share with your youngsters.

Cleverly written—and beautifully illustrated by his own hand—this book is the perfect coda to George's career, which ended upon his death on July 16, 2017 at age 77. George hadn't made a new movie in eight years, having been labelled "the zombie guy." In 2009, when I interviewed him for the last time for *Fangoria* magazine, he complained to me privately that it had become difficult for him to get non-zombie movies financed, due to his legacy typecasting. With the release of *The Little World of Humongo Bongo* by ChiZine Publications, your impression of George will undergo a major overhaul. (How did ChiZine know this work even existed, having only been published in Belgium two decades ago? Producer and *Rue Morgue* magazine vet

Dave Alexander's fascinating afterword interview with George reveals the book's origins.) With *The Little World of Humongo Bongo*, readers young and old, fans and non-fans, can experience a George A. Romero that not enough people knew during his lifetime: a warm, self-effacing, caring and happy man, with a heart the size of Humongo Bongo.

━━━●◆➤◆●━━━

Tony Timpone served as *Fangoria* magazine editor-in-chief from 1987–2010 before moving on to manage the company's Video on Demand and DVD divisions. As a co-host/producer, Timpone worked on *Fangoria Radio* for Sirius XM Satellite Radio for four years. In 2004, Timpone served as associate producer to Bravo's *100 Scariest Movie Moments*. Since 1998, he has been the Co-director of International Programming for Montreal's Fantasia Film Festival. Twitter: @tonytimpone1

On the wee little planet of Tongo, there once lived two Humongos. It was a good thing there weren't any more of them. There would hardly have been any room. Tongo is so very, very small and Humongos are gigantic. They are great, scaly things that breathe fire and eat leaves off the tops of the highest trees. (On the planet Earth, flamingos eat a lot of shrimp. That's what makes them pink. Humongos eat a lot of tree leaves, so they are green.)

One of the Humongos was named Pongo. He was two hundred years old. Being the oldest, he was thought of as the wisest by Humongo Bongo, who was the younger of the two.

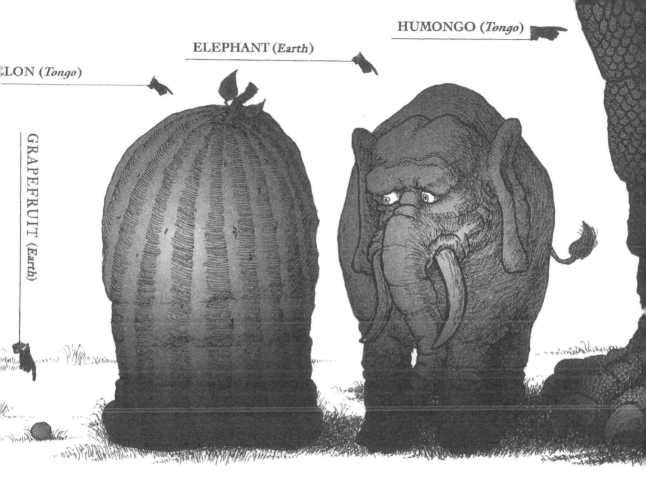

MELON (*Tongo*)

ELEPHANT (*Earth*)

HUMONGO (*Tongo*)

GRAPEFRUIT (*Earth*)

Bongo wasn't even a hundred yet. He was only ninety-eight.

They lived in Tongo's northern hemisphere in a beautiful lush Wood where a milk river flowed and where honey melons grew to be the size of elephants. (Bongo could hold a honey melon in one hand, the way a human on Earth might hold a grapefruit. That should give you some idea of just how big Humongos are.)

Neither of the two giants knew how they came to live on the planet Tongo. They supposed they had simply hatched there out of Humongo eggs. Having been there the longest, Pongo knew the ways of the place quite well, and Bongo was always asking him questions.

"What's a Humongo Being?"

"Why, you are, Bongo. And of course so am I."

"Are there others?"

"Not in this part of the universe. At least I've never seen any."

"Are we the last ones here? Or the first?"

"I expect that we are neither the first nor the last. I don't believe we're that special. We're just . . . here. Now. That's all that matters."

"What are we doing here?"

"Waiting."

"For what?"

"For the next thing to happen."

"How long will we have to wait?"

"As long as it takes."

"That's boring."

"Take a drink from the milkfall. Eat a honey melon. Enjoy the smell of the buddy blossoms and the pine. Listen to the song of the birds."

"The birds are so small, I can hardly hear them."

"You'd hear them better if you weren't asking questions all the time."

One day, with an impatient pout, Bongo said, "I don't want to just sit here and wait. I'm going to take a walk. To the edge of the Wood." And with that, he stood up and marched off through the trees.

He hadn't gotten very far when the thought of being alone began to frighten him. It was dark in the Wood. There were so many trees and they all looked the same. One could easily get lost. Bongo soon turned around and walked back toward the milkfall.

When he got there he found Pongo packing up a collection of tree-tops and filling empty honey melons with milk.

"What are you doing?" Bongo asked.

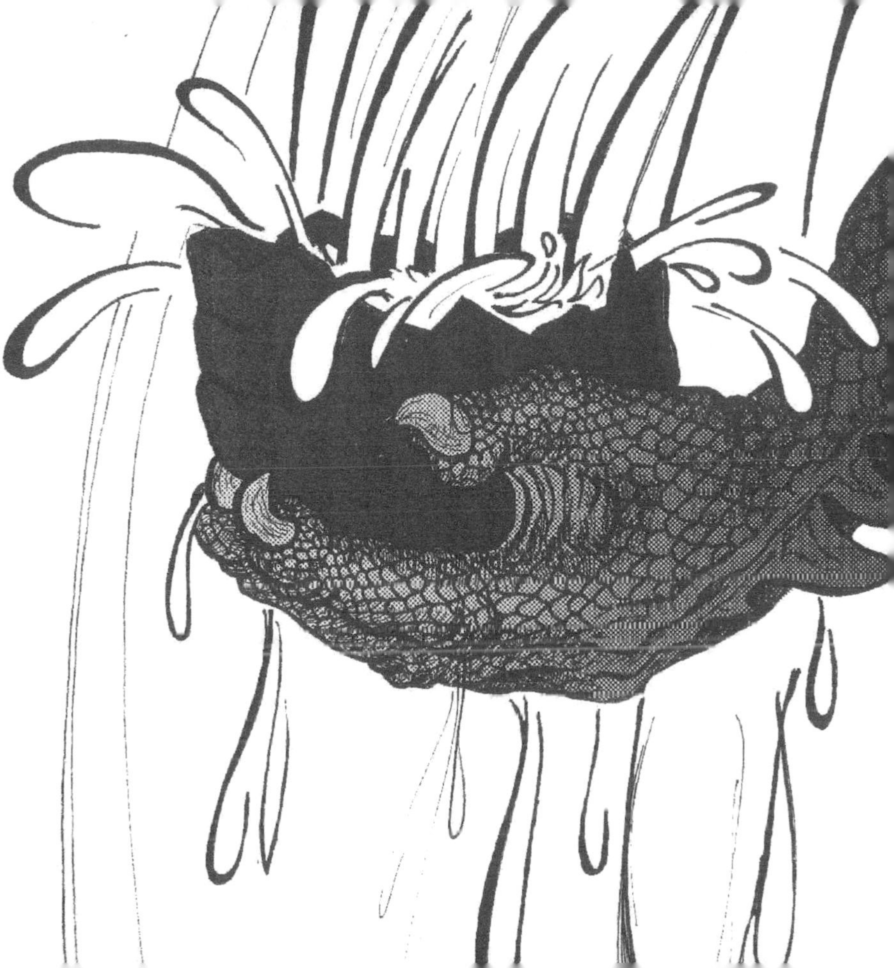

"I'm moving to the other side of the planet," replied Pongo.

"Why?"

"I fear there might be trouble."

Bongo was puzzled. "Trouble?" he said nervously.

"If you insist on walking to the edge of the Wood, you might…" Pongo hesitated and looked at his young companion. "Well, you might cause something to happen."

"But that's what we've been waiting for, isn't it? For something to happen?"

"Things are supposed to happen naturally. We're not supposed to cause them to happen." Pongo slung the tree-tops over his shoulder, gathered the melons full of milk and started off.

"Don't leave, Pongo. I'll be lonely. And afraid."

"You'll be fine," said Pongo. "You're old enough to be on your own."

"Please stay. I won't do it. I won't walk to the edge of the Wood."

"Yes you will. If not today, then someday soon. Don't worry," said Pongo, "the planet is so small that I'll be able to hear you from the other side. If there's a problem, just call. I'll be there. Waiting."

Pongo went lumbering off. Bongo listened to his footsteps. It wasn't long, only about ten minutes or so, before the footsteps stopped. Pongo had reached his destination. There was some rattling and some rustling (the sounds of Pongo setting down his tree-tops and melons). Then there was a loud THU-BUMP (the sound of Pongo sitting down to wait).

"Pongo? Are you on the other side?"

"I'm here, Bongo," came the reply, "all settled in."

Pongo had been right. The planet really was small enough to

hear things all the way from the other hemisphere, providing those things were loud enough. (Humongos are very, very loud.) Hearing Pongo's voice reassured Bongo and took away some of his fears.

Soon night came and Bongo, feeling lonely, fell asleep. At the same time, morning came on Pongo's side of the planet. Pongo spent the day waiting. When night came on Pongo's side, the morning sun woke Bongo from his dreams of adventure.

Bongo breathed in the dew mist which was flavored by the clean scent of pine and he found that he felt much better about things. Since nobody was talking, he heard the sweet bird song rising from around his feet far below and the cheerful sound made him much less lonely. After a breakfast of melons and milk, he was ready to try walking again.

He made a few wrong turns in among the trees, and he got lost once or twice, but he finally reached the edge of the Wood, and what he saw there was unlike anything he had ever dreamed of or imagined.

There were no trees outside the Wood, but there was a magnificent landscape of multi-coloured rock that rose to great peaks, taller than a Humongo, and then plunged suddenly into shaded valleys. The sun glistened off crystals, making them seem to spark. Long fingers of light stretched through cracks and faults in the stones. Friendly looking little clouds sprinkled rain into the deep canyons and, above them, rainbows came and went like the wings of giant butterflies. Humongo Bongo just stood there smiling for the rest of the day.

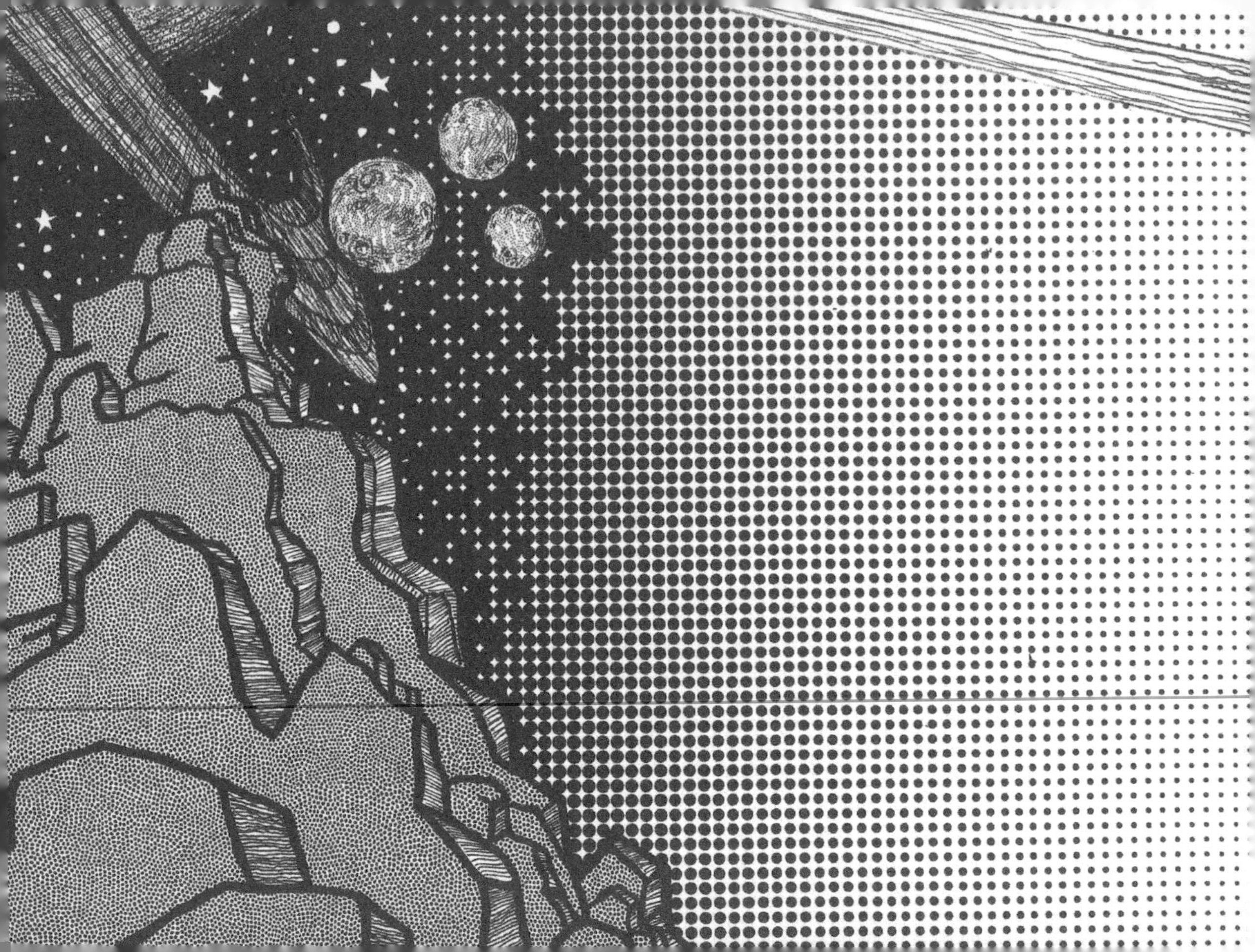

When night came, Tongo's three moons made everything shine silvery-blue. Stars came out by the hundreds, then by the thousands, then by the tens-of-thousands. Meteors streaked across the sky and the glow from Saturn's rings rose and fell like a dancer's skirt on the horizon. Bongo stood there all night gazing at all these wondrous new sights.

When the morning sun rose over the granite peaks, Bongo called out. "Pongo. I have walked to the edge of the Wood and I like it here. I like it a lot!"

"That's good, Bongo," Pongo called back. "I just hope there isn't any trouble."

There wasn't any trouble. There wasn't anything at all for three days and three nights. All that time, Bongo just stood in the same spot and watched the sky. Then, on the fourth day, Bongo looked down and noticed something moving slowly toward him on the pebbly ground below. (If he had been a Human on Earth, he might have thought it looked like a column of ants. There were ants on Tongo, but they were too small for Bongo to see so he didn't even know they existed.)

"Pongo," he cried. "There are some tiny, little creatures coming."

Pongo called back from the other side of the planet asking, "How many legs do they have? Eight? Six? Four?"

"It's hard to see. I think they have . . . yes, they have two legs. Like us."

"Just what I was afraid of."

"What do you mean? What are these creatures?"

"Peanuts."

"Peanuts?"

"The little ones of Tongo."

"Little ones? Well, they surely are little!"

"You should leave," called Pongo. "Come and join me here, on the other side. And make sure they don't follow you."

"Why? What is there to fear from little ones like these?"

"They often bring trouble. Come away before—"

Bongo interrupted him before he could finish. "Pongo! They seem to be . . . bringing me presents. Gifts. There's no trouble here. No trouble at all."

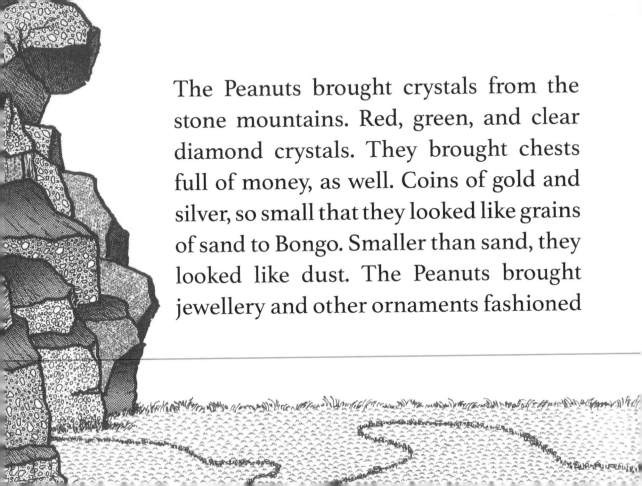

The Peanuts brought crystals from the stone mountains. Red, green, and clear diamond crystals. They brought chests full of money, as well. Coins of gold and silver, so small that they looked like grains of sand to Bongo. Smaller than sand, they looked like dust. The Peanuts brought jewellery and other ornaments fashioned from precious metals, and they brought great giant barrels of the grape juice that Peanuts loved to drink (on Earth it's called wine). They had made the barrels specially for the occasion. To them, the barrels were the size of ocean-going ships. To Bongo, they were the size of thimbles.

"They want to be friends, Pongo! They . . . they must like me!"

"They're afraid of you."

"But . . . how can that be? I've done them no harm. I've done no harm to anybody or anything on this planet . . . excepting, of course, the melons and the tree-top leaves which will all grow back. Why would these Peanuts ever be afraid of me?"

"Because they are Peanuts, and you are a Humongo."

Bongo thought that was nonsense. Looking at the Peanuts, he gently tapped his chest and said, "Bongo. Bongo. My name is Bongo." Because of the way he tapped his chest the Peanuts seemed to understand that he was identifying himself. They spread out in a circle and began to sing in a language that Bongo had never heard before.

"HUMONGO BONGO RONGO TONGO DEI! HUMONGO BONGO RONGO TONGO DEI!"

The words sounded funny but the melody they chanted was quite pleasant. Soothing, like a lullaby. Bongo sat on the ground and leaned back against trees at the edge of the Wood. It felt good. He'd been standing there for four days and nights. (Humongos are very heavy so you can imagine how tired their feet must get when they stand in one spot for a long time.)

The Peanuts continued their chanting until the sun started to drop behind the stone mountains. Bongo played with the treasures they'd brought him, letting them sift through his fingers and fall over his belly (the way an Earth child might play with sand on the beach). He tasted the grape juice but found that he didn't like it and it made his stomach feel funny so he spilled it out. Reaching back into the Wood, he picked a ripe honey melon and snapped off a tree-top. This made a tremendously loud sound which terrified the little Peanuts. They stopped singing and broke out of the circle they had formed. Some of them started to run back toward the rocks.

"Don't run away," said Bongo, looking disappointed. "I'm not going to hurt you. I'm just big and noisy."

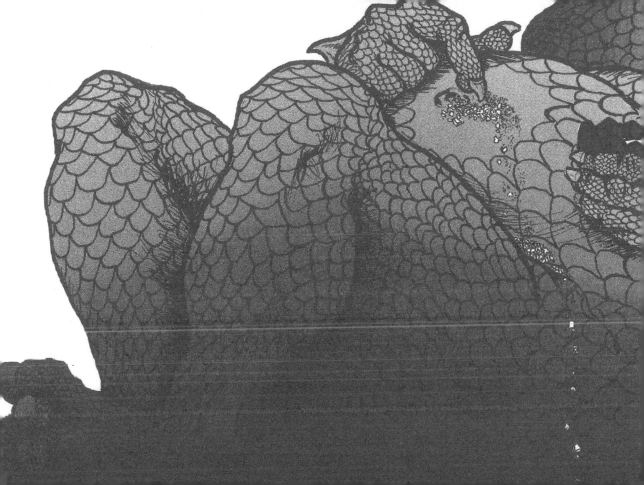

The Peanuts didn't understand Humongo Bongo's language any more than he understood theirs. To them his great booming voice sounded like thunder. They backed farther away, not knowing what to expect. But after a time, when they saw that the giant creature wasn't coming after them, they slowly returned.

Bongo ate his melon and nibbled on his tree-top. A tributary of the milk river flowed near enough for him to reach. He scooped at it with the empty melon rind and took a cool drink. Then he played with the treasure for a short while more, enjoying the way it sparkled when it caught the red rays of the setting sun.

Soon the Wood crickets began to chirp and the sun

disappeared behind the mountains. As the sky darkened with the coming of night, the Peanuts began to sing again.

"HUMONGO BONGO RONGO TONGO DEI!"

There's no trouble here, thought Bongo, but he didn't say it out loud for fear of frightening his little visitors again. *No trouble at all. This is nice. This is very nice indeed.* And that was his last thought before he fell into a deep, contented sleep.

Humongo Bongo stayed there at the edge of the Wood (which was also the edge of the Rocky Ridge where the Peanuts lived) for a very long time. He stopped counting the days and nights after forty-seven of each had passed. When he woke up on the forty-eighth day, he couldn't remember whether the next number was supposed to be forty-eight or forty-nine. He called out and asked Pongo, but Pongo had not been counting the days and nights so he wasn't able to offer any help.

"It doesn't matter, I guess," said Bongo. "I don't really need to know how many days go by. I'll just enjoy each one as it comes."

Every afternoon the Peanuts brought more treasures, and every evening as the sun turned red they sang Humongo Bongo to sleep. *What a wonderful life I have here,* thought Bongo. *This is much better than sitting in the Wood and waiting for something to happen. I'm not even lonely. I have my friends, the Peanuts, and I can talk to Pongo whenever I want to. I feel like I could stay here forever!*

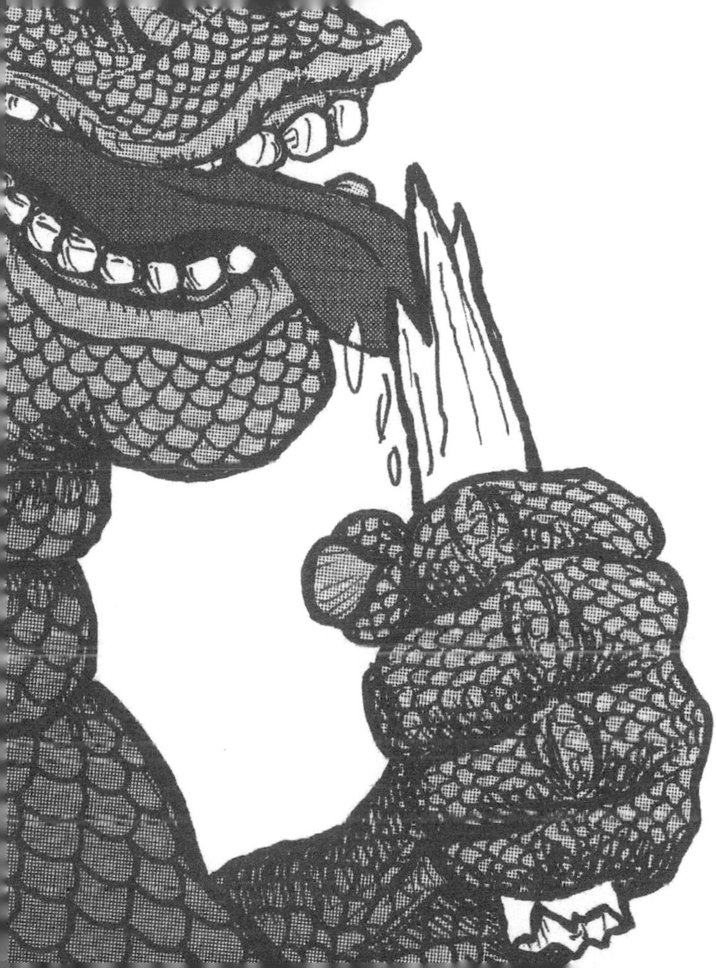

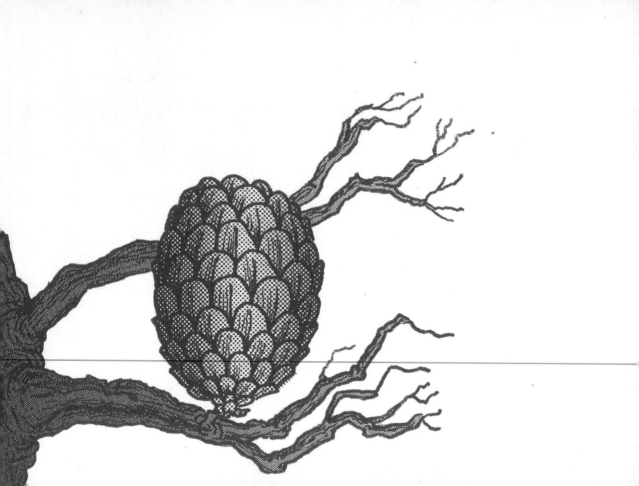

After thirty more days and nights, which Bongo did not bother to count, the first winds of winter started to blow. The air grew cold. The trees in the Wood lost their leaves. The honey melons shrivelled and dropped to the ground. None of this bothered Humongo Bongo. He had plenty of blubber to keep him warm, and his scaly hide kept him from feeling the cold winds except for right around his nose. The river turned to iced milk but Bongo was able to break off chunks from the surface and lick them (the way Earthlings lick the things they call Popsicles).

Before long, the trees began to produce their winter crop of pine-butter-cones which Bongo looked forward to every year. He thought that pine-butter-cones were almost as delicious as honey melons, and since they only came in deep winter they were a very special treat.

Things were just fine, if you happened to be a Humongo, that is. Things were not so fine if you happened to be a Peanut. The Peanuts didn't have thick, green hides to keep them warm, and the few crops that sustained them, the grapes and the dilly weeds which turned black and pruney with the first frost of winter, wouldn't produce again until springtime.

One very cold day, when the Peanuts came with their gifts, Bongo noticed that they looked different. They were so small and so far away down there on the ground that he couldn't see them clearly enough to tell what the difference was exactly, so he sat up and leaned forward.

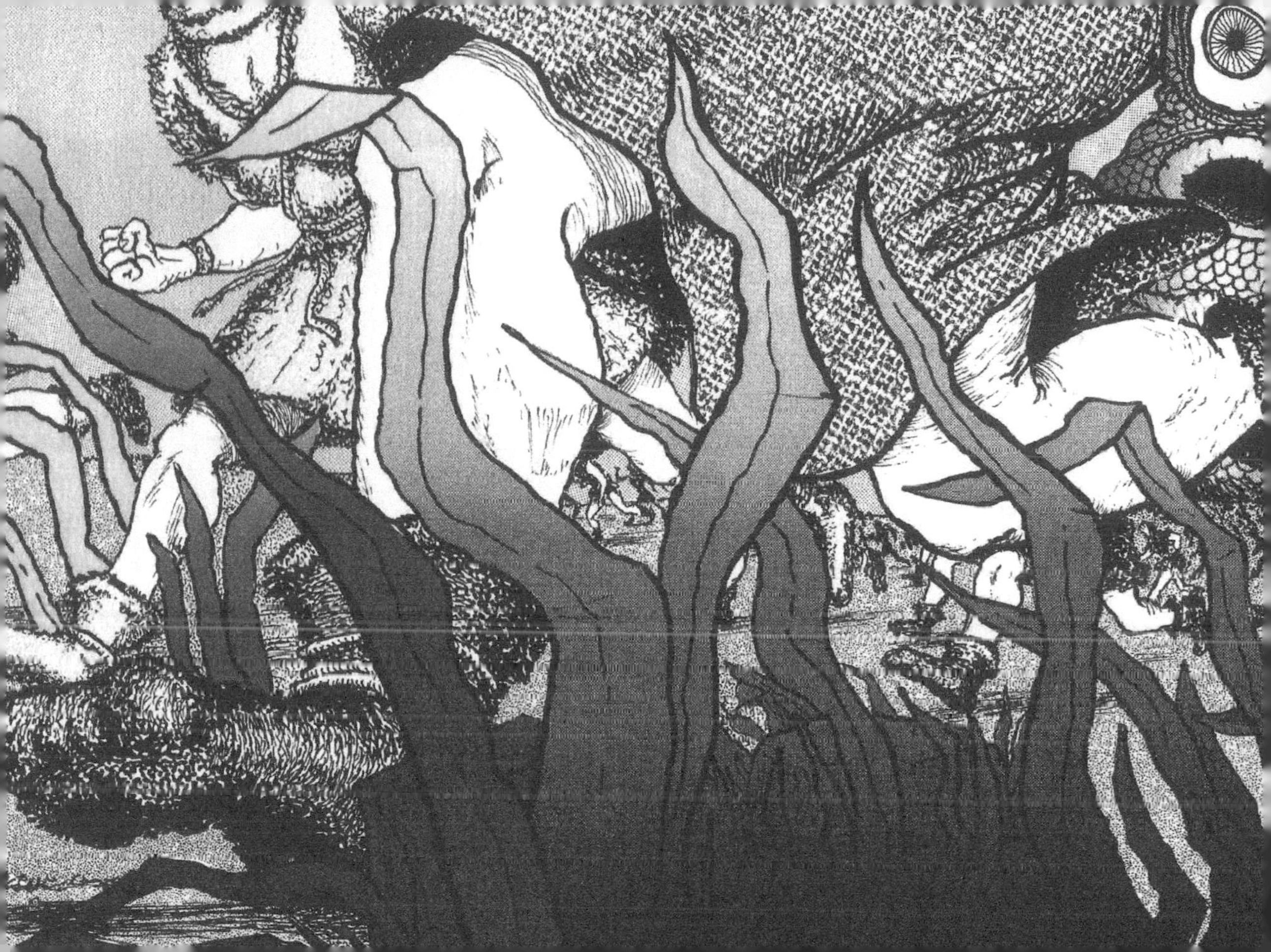

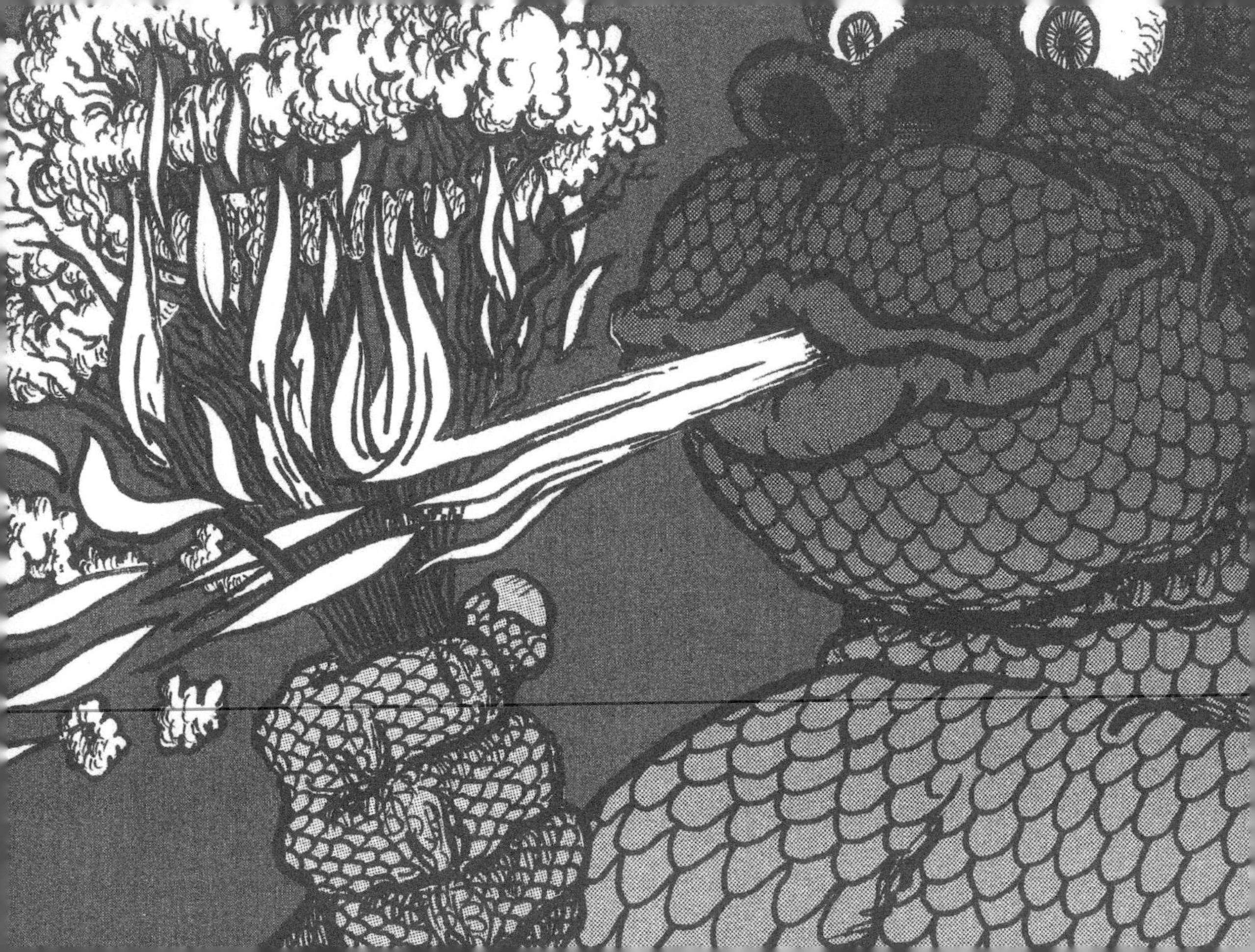

This sent the Peanuts into a panic. They dropped what they were carrying and ran screaming back into the rocks. But Bongo managed to get a closer look at some of them. Their little bodies were covered. That's what made them look different. They were bundled up in old rags and grape leaves and marble moss that was tied on with vines. Clouds of vapour puffed out of their mouths and noses when they breathed. And they were trembling, not because they were afraid, but because they were freezing cold.

Humongo Bongo sat up straight again. He knew how he could help. He reached quickly back into the Wood and broke off a handful of bare tree-tops. Holding them up in front of his mouth, he tightened his throat to close off his windpipe. He relaxed the acid glands on the roof of his mouth and he blew out a short but powerful breath. A fiery jet came rocketing out with a tremendous roar and the tree-tops in his hand caught fire.

He set the burning timbers down carefully on the rocky side of the border, making sure that the flames never touched the rest of the Wood. Then he leaned back against the trees and remained still.

After a while a few brave Peanuts came out of the rocks and moved cautiously toward the fire. Bongo could tell that the warmth felt good to them. Over the next few hours, more Peanuts came. They brought sticks and touched the tips of each to the outer edges of the flame.

The sticks caught fire and, holding them up like torches, the Peanuts hurried back into the rocks, bringing little bits of warmth back to the hidden places where they dwelled.

Bongo's tree-tops burned out before long. The ashes cooled and blew away on the wind. But it didn't matter. The Peanuts had little fires of their own now, and by adding more twigs and vines whenever the flames got low they could keep them burning for the rest of the winter. For the rest of time, if they were careful.

That evening as the sun set, Bongo could see

flickering crowns of warm orange light rising from caves and crevasses throughout the Rocky Ridge

and he knew he had done a helpful thing.

Carrying torches, the Peanuts returned just as night was about to fall. They formed a circle and sang their strange little song until Bongo fell asleep.

"HUMONGO BONGO RONGO TONGO DEI!"

Life went on without any major incidents for another two months or so. The cold winds surrendered to a drizzly spring. The milk river thawed and resumed its lazy flow and soon the Peanuts didn't need the fires anymore. They kept them burning just the same. They didn't dare let them die because they knew that another winter would come, and another after that, and so on.

One day, as afternoon darkened into evening, Bongo realized that the Peanuts had not come out of the rocks with their usual gifts. When the Wood crickets began to chirp there was no little song to accompany them. Bongo had a hard time falling asleep because he was troubled by the silence. He wondered if something bad had happened to his tiny friends.

The next evening was just as quiet. No Peanuts, no gifts. Just silence. *Where are they?* Bongo wondered. *I hope they're alright.*

As night fell, Bongo could see the flickering orange lights in amongst the rocks. That meant the fires were still burning. That meant the Peanuts were tending them, adding wood when the flames got low. That meant they were still alive, which made Bongo feel better. But only a little better. Why didn't they come with their presents and their song?

Three more evenings passed with no sign of the Peanuts. Bongo was really getting worried. *Maybe they're sick*, he thought. *Maybe they need help. I'll walk onto the Rocky Ridge and check. No. That would probably frighten them. I might even step on some of them in the dark. Oh . . . I don't like this at all. I don't understand why things have suddenly changed.*

The next day, he called out to Pongo, "Why have the Peanuts stopped bringing me presents?"

"Maybe they have nothing left to give."

"Nothing left? How can that be? They couldn't have given me . . . everything." An uncomfortable thought came suddenly. "Oh, my goodness. That's what you think, isn't it, Pongo? You think they gave me everything that they had!"

"It's been a long time. And they've been bringing you presents every day."

"Oh, that makes me feel awful. I've gone and wasted all of their grape juice. I spilled it out because I didn't like the way it tasted. And all the nice shiny things they gave me. I've just been playing with them as though they were bits of sand. Now the poor Peanuts are left with nothing!"

Then Bongo got an idea. "I know! I'll give it all back. Not the grape juice, that's gone into the ground, but the shiny things . . . I can give those back!"

The shiny things were scattered all around. Silver coins, golden jewellery, gemstones, and pearls were scrunched into the ground where Bongo had been sitting on them and sleeping on them. He knew they were down there because he could see little edges of them glistening in the sunlight, but they were mostly covered with dirt or hidden in among the blades of new spring grass. They were so teeny-tiny small that he couldn't pick them up one at a time, his enormous fingers were far too big. He thought he could scoop them up in batches, but each time he tried, his clumsy Humongo hands came up with mostly pebbles and bits of earth. (Imagine a human trying to pick up motes of dust.) He soon gave up, realizing it was impossible.

"I could tell the Peanuts to come and collect the shiny things themselves. No. My voice scares them. And besides, there's a language problem."

Bongo slumped back against the trees feeling guilty and helpless. *I miss them*, he thought. *I miss those little Peanuts. I like them to come and visit me. They're cute. Fun to watch. I don't need presents. I never wanted them in the first place. It was their idea to bring them. Now I've gone and wasted everything and they have nothing left. If they would only just come back and sing that silly song. They'd soon see that I don't need to get presents. And maybe they would like me again.*

More days passed in silence. Spring rain fell every morning. Bongo kept dry by huddling under the trees, but the rain had a funny way of making him feel even gloomier than he felt before.

"What are you doing, Pongo?" he called.

"Waiting," came the reply.

"Yes," said Bongo. "Me too."

Then one morning Bongo was awakened by a series of sharp little pains in his legs. Not terrible pains, they felt like bee stings, but they hurt badly enough for him to sit up and shout, "Ouch!"

On the other side of the planet, Pongo heard the shout and called back: "What is it, Bongo?"

"I . . . I don't know," Bongo answered. Then he looked down and was amazed by what he saw.

All around the edge of the Wood the Peanuts were jumping up and down, shouting, and trying to look fierce. Their faces were painted with bright streaks of colour. They carried war shields made from bits of slate and decorated with angry-looking designs. They had bows and arrows, spears, and slingshots that hurled stones. They were attacking!

The spears and arrows didn't fly very high, none higher than Humongo Bongo's knees, but they stuck, like splinters, in his shins and ankles and toes.

"Ouch! OUCH! OUUUUUUUUUCH!!!" Bongo cried, and he stood up suddenly, blocking the sun with his massive shoulders.

Looking up at the giant Humongo, the Peanuts lost most of their bravery. With a final desperate volley of rocks and arrows, they retreated into the mountains and disappeared.

Bongo was stunned. He sat down again and tried to pull the splinters out of his legs. The spears were big enough for him to pick out with his fingers, but the arrows were so tiny that when he tried to get them he only pushed them in deeper.

"OOOUUUUUUUUCCCCHHHH!!!!!"

"Do you need help, Bongo?" Pongo called from the other side.

"No. I'm alright."

"What happened?"

"The Peanuts. They . . . attacked me! With sticks and arrows and stones."

"I thought it might be something like that."

"Why did they do it, Pongo? I haven't done anything to them. I'm the same as I always was. Why don't they like me anymore? Why do they want to hurt me all of a sudden? It's because of the presents, isn't it? Because they gave me everything and now they have nothing left for themselves."

"That's part of the reason, I'm sure," said Pongo, "but not all of it. No, even if you had been able to give everything back to them, I'm afraid they might still be trying to hurt you now."

"Why? What do they want?"

"They want the Wood."

"The Wood?"

"Until you walked to the edge, the Wood was a dark and mysterious place to the Peanuts. They never dared to enter it for fear of what terrible creatures they might find there. Their imaginations made them dream of monsters far more terrifying than we Humongos. Then you came out of the trees and they saw you for the first time. They were afraid of you, but not as afraid as they were of the things in their dreams. They brought you presents so you would leave them alone, and after a while, they got used to you."

"But I've been nice to them. And I always left them alone. I even helped them. I gave them fire to keep warm in the winter time."

"That's precisely why they've gotten so brave. The Wood is not a dark and mysterious place to them anymore. They once imagined it to be filled with monsters. Now they imagine it to be filled with bountiful treasures that you want to keep secret from them. They believe that's why you're sitting there. They think you're guarding the entrance to a fabulous new realm."

"That's ridiculous! I'm not guarding anything! If there were bountiful treasures, I'd be happy to share them. I'm always happy to share. Why . . . I'll give the Peanuts anything they want!"

"They can't rely on that. You might change your mind one day. Besides, the Peanuts are too proud to take gifts."

"But they gave me gifts!"

"Yes. Until they had nothing left. And now they want the secret treasures which they believe you are keeping hidden in the Wood."

"How do you know all these things, Pongo?"

"Once, a long time ago . . . before you hatched out of your egg, before your egg even existed . . . this very same thing happened to me. That's why I knew there'd be trouble if you walked to the edge."

Just as Pongo said this, a second attack came. The Peanuts ran out of their rock shelters and, shouting ferociously, charged at Humongo Bongo, shooting arrows, throwing stones, and hurling spears.

"OOOOOOOOOOUUUUUUUUCCCCCHHHHH!!!!!!"

Bongo cried as ten, then twenty, then thirty more splinters flew into his legs. "I don't like this! I'm going back into the Wood!"

"They'll only come after you," warned Pongo.

"What else can I do?" Bongo pleaded with pain in his voice.

"You can destroy them," Pongo answered calmly.

"Destroy the Peanuts?"

"It can be done easily. By breathing your fire on them."

"I . . . I could never . . ."

"I know," said Pongo. "Neither could I."

"OOOOOUUUUCCCCCCCCCHHHHH!!!!!" screamed Bongo as a hundred more splinters stabbed into him.

Made even braver by the fact that the Humongo wasn't fighting back, the Peanuts were attacking with inspired fury. Bongo's legs were starting to look like they had suddenly grown little wooden hairs.

Pongo's voice remained calm and reassuring. He knew from experience that the Peanuts couldn't really harm Bongo. The spears and arrows hurt, certainly, but the pain would go away and the rains would wash out the splinters over time. There was no real danger. So Pongo stayed on the other side of the planet and said, "If you don't want to destroy them, Bongo, you're left with only one choice. Step aside and let them have the Wood."

"Of course," said Bongo. "Why didn't I think of that?"

When Humongo Bongo stood up, the Peanuts cringed away from him as they had done before, though their new found bravery kept them from retreating into the mountains. They continued their assault, hurling rocks and shooting arrows, but because they had dropped back, the missiles fell short. Only one or two of the arrows reached Bongo's toes. He stepped aside just the same, moving away from his attackers.

Three great, hundred-yard strides took him far away from the place where he'd been sitting for so long. Far away from the trees. Far away from the honey melons and the milk river. Far away from the Peanut treasure that lay scrunched into the earth at the edge of two worlds.

He found himself in the outer reaches of the Rocky Ridge. He turned around and sat on a slab of granite. Then he waved his hand, in a welcoming gesture, inviting the Peanuts to enter the Wood.

A victorious cheer rose from the little people. They hugged one another and danced around in circles for a long time. Bongo couldn't help but smile when he saw such happiness. Then, bringing their fire torches and what few remaining possessions they had left, the Peanuts moved into the darkening Wood, singing as they went. Only now their song was slightly different.

"HUMONGO BONGO RONGO VINCI TEI! HUMONGO BONGO RONGO VINCI TEI!"

Silence fell and Bongo's smile slowly faded. For a time he sat there on the stone, picking splinters from his legs which were now itching mightily. The sun dropped behind the mountains and, as night fell, he could see flickering crowns of orange light rising from amidst the pines in the Wood.

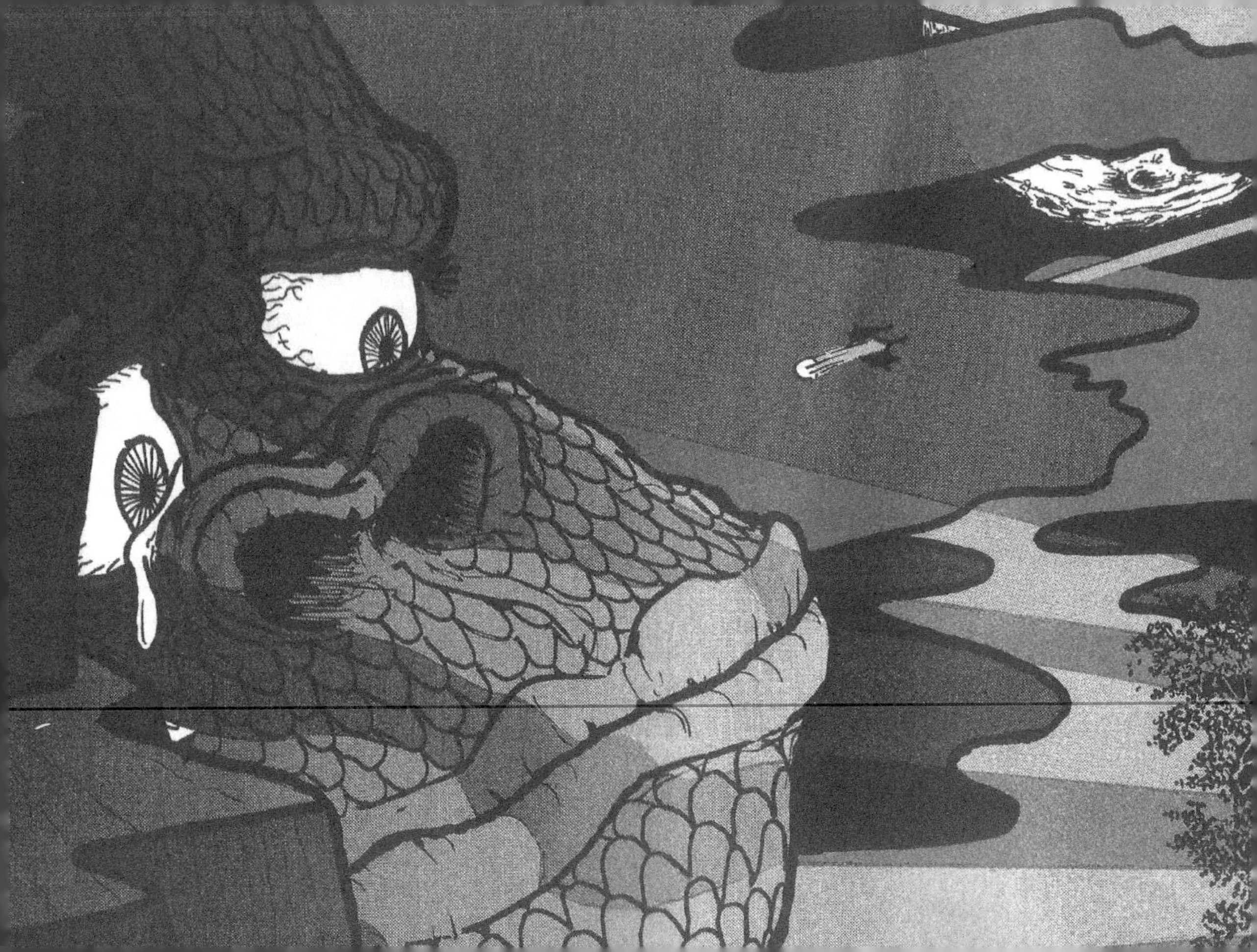

I hope they're careful, he thought. *I hope they don't set fire to any of the honey melon bushes.*

He suddenly felt like crying. It was all so unfair. He thought of talking to Pongo but he decided against it. He was feeling . . . He didn't know what he was feeling. He'd never been embarrassed before, never been humiliated.

That's what he was feeling. Humiliation. Only he didn't know it. He only knew that he hadn't done anything terribly wrong. Certainly not on purpose. He could have destroyed the Peanuts but he didn't. He had only wanted to have a nice time. If only he hadn't wasted all of their presents, maybe things would be different.

He spent the night on that granite slab. When morning came he tried to pick the remaining splinters out of his shins, but it was impossible. When the sun was high at noontime he stood up and began to wander among the stones of his new world.

The Rocky Ridge seemed a very unwelcoming place to Humongo Bongo. Sharp boulders cut into the soles of his feet and his elbows scraped on the sheer walls of marble mountains.

Before long, he came upon an orchard which the Peanuts had carefully planted with grapes. He realized that he was hungry.

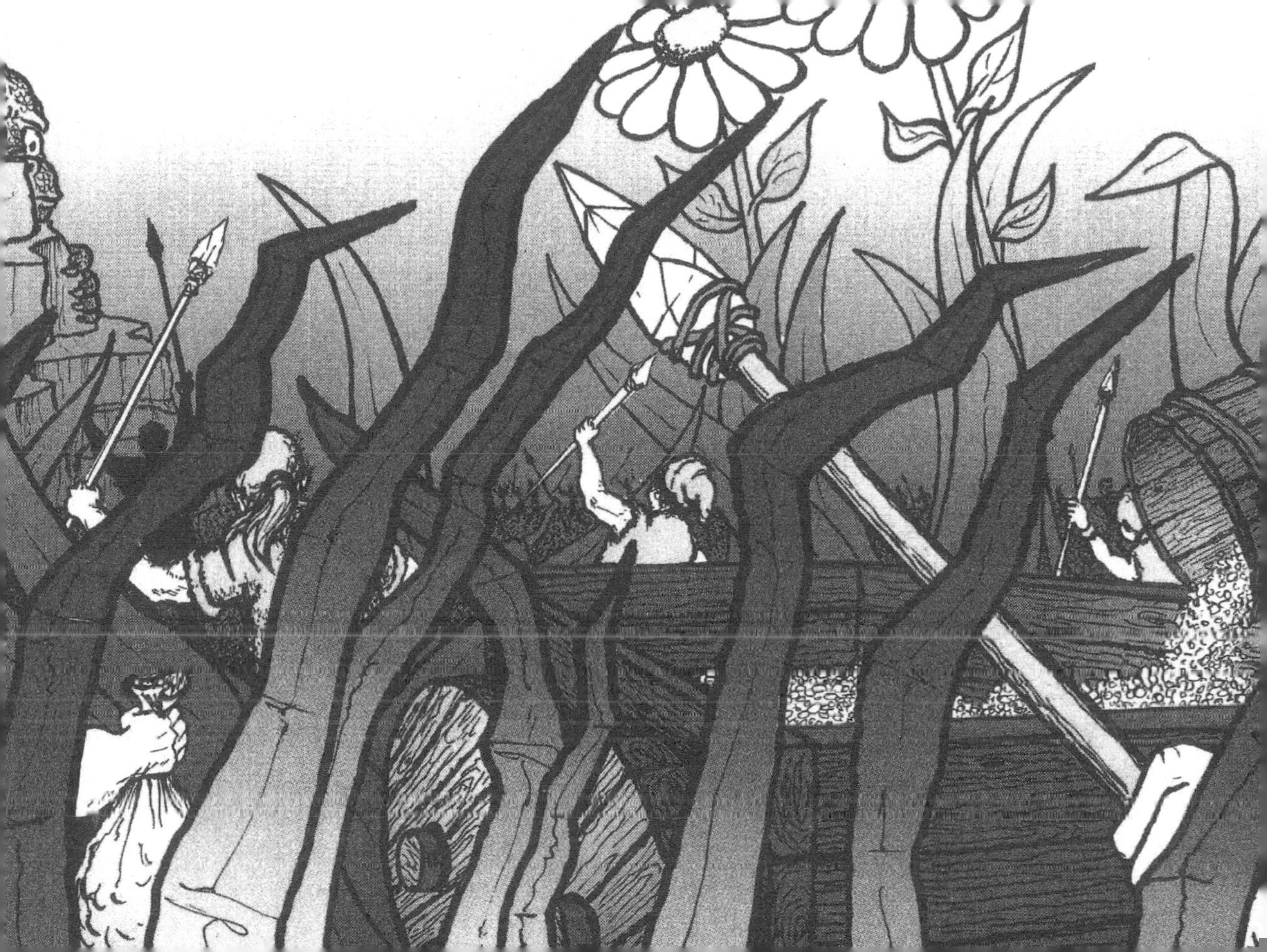

He reached down and tried to pick some of the fruit from the vines but his clumsy hands were too big. The grapes squished, leaving sticky juices. When he tried to lick his fingers clean, his lips puckered from the awful taste. He saw a little patch of dilly weed and discovered that it was big enough for him to pull it from the rocks. When he tried to eat it, he found it too bitter to be worth the while.

Just before the sun set it started to rain very hard. Bongo wasn't used to being wet. In the Wood, he was always able to crouch under the trees when it rained. He looked around for shelter and he noticed a cave where a family of Peanuts once dwelled. He peeked inside, but it was too dark to see anything. He tried to reach his hand through the opening but it was so small that even his pinky-finger couldn't squeeze its way through.

He wasn't suited for the Rocky Ridge. No, he wasn't at all suited for this hard, unfriendly, dreary, bitter, wet place. He sat down sadly and rested his head on the side of a mountain. He saw the distant glow of the fires in the Wood. The trees, like giant umbrellas, were keeping those fires dry and burning. He started to cry, but he couldn't feel the tears on his cheeks because they got all mixed in with the falling raindrops.

The next day, Bongo wandered back toward the entrance to the Wood. Noticing some activity on his side of the border he moved closer and saw that the Peanuts were hard at work right at the very spot where Bongo had been sitting for so many months. Using rakes and burrows they were gathering up the treasure that Bongo had scrunched into the ground.

Good, thought Bongo. *They'll get their treasure back and maybe they won't think so badly of me anymore.* He took another step closer and was sorry that he did.

"OOOOOOUUUUUUUUUUUUUHHHHHHHHHH!!!!!!" he shouted as the first spears hit his legs. These spears were bigger, heavier, sharper than the ones the Peanuts had used before. These new ones had been carved from sturdy tree limbs in the Wood.

A band of Peanut warriors had gathered to protect the workers who were busy collecting the treasure. They were scowling and shouting and they looked fiercer than ever. Confidence, and of course their heavy new weapons, had made them bold.

"They're not afraid of you anymore," came Pongo's voice from the other hemisphere. "They're not afraid of you at all. They beat you once. They feel that they can do it again."

"They didn't beat me! I stepped aside because I didn't want to fight!"

"They don't see it that way."

"OOOOOOUUUUUUUUUUUUUUHHHHHHHHHH!!!!!!"

"Punish them," said Pongo, his voice still calm. "Step on them. Steal some of their women. Eat a few of their babies."

"That's GROSS!" said Bongo, backing far enough away so that the spears could no longer reach him.

"Set fire to the Wood. Then no one will have it."

"That's STUPID!"

"I don't know what else to suggest, except for . . . waiting."

"That's BORING!" Bongo shouted. He was getting very irritated. "All you ever want to do is waste your time WAITING! Waiting for WHAT?!"

"For the next thing to happen. The Peanuts won't stay in the Wood very long. They'll find that they don't like it there, just as their elders did a long time ago. Peanuts have a taste for grape juice and dilly weed."

"YUCK!" said Bongo. "Dilly weed is sour! Grape juice makes my stomach get all gurgly and loud!"

"Milk and honey melons probably do the same to the Peanut people. Wait and see what happens. Just . . . wait."

More time passed. Humongo Bongo spent his days wandering through the rocks hoping to find something interesting or at least something pretty to sit and look at for a while.

Strange, he thought. *When I was sitting at the edge of the Wood, the Rocky Ridge looked pretty. Especially when the sun set over the tops of the mountains. Now I think it looks ugly. Hard, unfriendly, dreary, bitter, wet. There's nothing about it that is in any way . . . INTERESTING!*

He never wandered far. He always stayed within sight of the edge where the Rocky Ridge met the Wood. He could see the milk river stream. That made him thirsty. He could see the honey melons hanging from the trees. That made him hungry. He could also see movement, on his side of the border, where the Peanuts were working to recover their treasure, and he knew that the warriors, with their heavy new spears, were sure to be there as well, ready to protect the workers. So he never got too close.

He drank rain water and ate dilly weed. The rain water didn't taste bad. It didn't taste like anything at all. The dilly weed was very, very sour, but after a few days he found that it didn't bother him to eat it. He didn't like it, but it didn't bother him, and he had to eat something.

At the end of each day he would try to find a suitable place to sleep. He tried a new spot every night, but none of them were comfortable. He'd squirm and wiggle and try to make his body fit in between the sharp edges of the rocks. He never fell asleep quickly, the rocks hurt him too much, and he had too many confusing thoughts in his mind. He felt homesick, lonely, guilty, and angry, all at the same time. Those weren't good feelings to have, even if you only had one of them. To have them all together was unbearable.

He didn't even have the stars to cheer him up. The dark clouds of springtime almost always kept them hidden. Now and again he'd catch a glimpse of one or two of them. One night he saw a meteor streak by. It was the only one he ever saw the whole time he was in the Rocky Ridge. He never saw all three moons at once. On a good night he'd see the first, or the second, or the third, one at a time, and only for a brief second or two, when a clear spot would move across the sky allowing one of them to peek through. The rest of the time, all he could see of the moons were fuzzy, dim ghosts, barely glowing behind the overcast sky.

"That makes it worse," he said to Pongo. "The moons glowing like that. It just reminds me of the days when I could see all three of them clearly. It's as if the clouds are saying, 'The moons are up here, alright, but you can't have them because they're not yours anymore!' Just like the milk and the honey melons. I can see them but I can't have them, because they're not mine anymore!"

The last thing he looked at every night was the flickering orange light that rose from amidst the trees in the Wood. And every night his last thoughts were the same. *Those mean old Peanuts. They're comfortable and I'm not. It isn't fair. It just isn't fair.* Then he would fall asleep because his body wouldn't let him stay awake any longer.

One morning something awakened him with a start. He wasn't sure exactly what it was. When he opened his eyes he saw . . . nothing. Absolutely nothing. Whiteness. Bright, hot whiteness. He realized that he was staring up into the eastern sky. He was staring directly at the sun. He turned away and blinked his eyes several times. After a moment he was able to see things again. There were spots in his eyes but he could make out the rocks, the mountains, the faults and crevasses.

The wetness was gone. The rocks were dry and brightly coloured. The mountains were casting long shadows across the Rocky Ridge. The rainy spring was over and summertime had arrived. Bongo's heart nearly jumped out of his body with joy. It must have been the sun, the early summer sun, that had awakened him so suddenly.

No sooner did he have that thought than something else attracted his attention. Chanting. Peanut voices rising in spirited song. Bongo looked toward the edge of the Wood. The Peanuts were gathering there, all of them. Their faces were painted. They were drumming on their shields, and stamping their spears in rhythm with the chant they were singing.

"HUMONGO BONGO RONGO VINCI TEI! HUMONGO BONGO RONGO VINCI TEI!"

It wasn't the sun that had awakened him. It was that awful chanting. As quickly as Bongo's heart had risen with the promise of summer, now it sank down, down, down into his shins, his ankles, his toes, which he feared would soon again be feeling the angry sting of spears and arrows and rocks from Peanut slingshots.

All at once, their courage mustered, the little people came storming out of the Wood, shouting and waving their weapons. The warriors ran in front. Behind them came the workers and the women, the children and the ones who were too old to fight, bearing with them all of the tribe's possessions. They had made wagons from lumber in the Wood and they had loaded them with chests that contained the coins and the jewels and the other shiny things they had salvaged. They were leaving the Wood, just as Pongo had predicted. They wanted to come back to the Rocky Ridge.

Bongo just stood there watching as the Peanuts came across the edge between the worlds and ran toward him over the stones. They were too far away for their weapons to reach him, but they were getting closer every minute. Bongo felt angrier than he had ever felt before in his ninety-eight years of life.

It's not fair, he thought. *None of this is fair! First they wanted the Wood. I gave it to them. Now they want the Rocky Ridge back. I don't want the Rocky Ridge but I'm not going to just give it to them! Not this time! Let them try to take it! Just let them TRY!*

The Peanuts got closer and closer. The first of their arrows stuck into the ground very near Bongo's feet. Then a sharp stone from a slingshot hit his big toe. Then a heavy wooden spear stabbed him in the ankle.

"OOOOOOOOOOOUUUUUUUUUCCCCCCH HHHHHHHHHH!!!!!!!!!"

Rage suddenly hardened Bongo's heart. He roared as loudly as he could and, using the scariest face he knew how to make, he glared angrily at the little people, but that didn't stop them. They kept on coming. They were confident of victory.

Bongo tightened his throat to close off his windpipe. He relaxed the acid glands on the roof of his mouth. He took a deep breath, puckered his lips, and leaned forward.

One powerful breath, he thought, *and they won't be Peanuts anymore. They'll be ashes in a fire storm. And soon those ashes will be blown away by the wind and the Peanuts will be gone . . . FOREVER!*

He didn't do it. He couldn't do it. It just wasn't in him.

Swallowing his rage . . . and the fire in his throat . . . he turned and ran away. Not from the Peanuts. Not from the sting of their weapons, but from the sting of the bad feelings inside himself. The anger, the confusion. He ran from the Rocky Ridge, a place which, from that day on, would always remind him of how terrible it felt to have your heart hardened by rage.

He ran and ran. From behind him came cheers from the tribe of little people and the taunting sound of their victorious song.

"HUMONGO BONGO RONGO VINCI TEI!"

He didn't hear it for long. His giant legs carried him swiftly over the horizon. Humongo voices can be heard from far, far away, but Peanut voices are so soft, even when they're shouting, that they can only be heard by someone very nearby. Soon Bongo could hear no sound at all, except for the stomping of his own wounded feet.

As he crossed to the other side of the stone mountains,

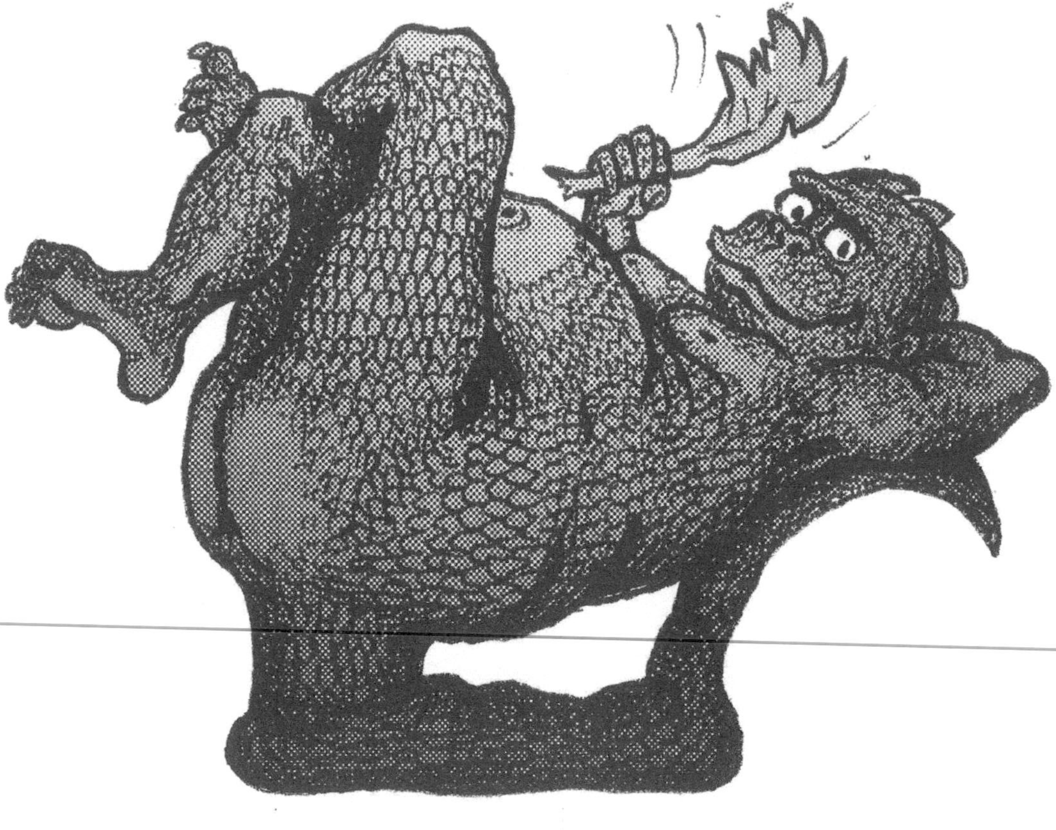

he stopped running and slowed to a walk. He walked, and walked, and walked, trying not to think of how sad he was.

Within a few minutes he found himself on the other side of the planet, and there was Pongo, relaxing in a field of tall purple grass, using a big purple leaf to fan away the heat of the summer sun.

"Pongo," said Bongo. "I didn't realize I'd walked so far. Is this the other hemisphere?"

"Yes it is. Good to see you, Bongo."

"Oh, you don't know how good it is to see you!"

Bongo sat down and Pongo helped him pick the splinters out of his ankles and toes. It made Bongo feel better. Not just getting the spears and arrows out of his hide, but being close to someone who was his own size, his own kind, someone who liked him and welcomed his company.

After a time, Bongo looked around and his mouth fell open. He hadn't noticed much of anything before that moment. He had been so full of bad thoughts that the only thing he had seen clearly was Pongo. Now he realized how beautiful everything looked here on the other side of the planet. The land stretched out in a flat plain that was carpeted with tall purple grass all the way to the outer edge of the horizon where it touched the sky. The grass swirled gently in the breeze making ever-changing patterns with its shades of colour that ranged from deep, dark burgundy to light, bright magenta. There were purple cactus plants and little purple plum fruits growing here and there, and there was a purple brook that meandered cheerfully on its long curvy way in and around purple cattails.

Pongo gave Bongo some plum fruits and dipped a handful of purple puddle pudding up from the bottom of the brook.

"Why . . . this place seems fabulous!" said Bongo.

"It's alright, I suppose," said Pongo. "But I miss the milk and the honey melons from the Wood."

Bongo tasted the plum fruit and then the pudding. Not as sour as dilly weed, but not nearly as sweet as a honey melon.

"And it's too hot here," Pongo went on.

"There's no shade. Nothing to rest your head on at night, the cactus plants are too prickly. And the colour purple gets really, really tiresome after you've been here for a while. It isn't like home, Bongo. No sir, it surely isn't anything like home."

"Things have gone terribly for us, haven't they, Pongo?" said Bongo remembering the old days in the shade of sheltering pines. (He didn't say this next part out loud, but he thought it privately: *It's all because of me. All because I got restless and wanted to walk to the edge of the Wood.*)

A month went by on the Purple Plain before Bongo heard a sound that he had hoped he would never hear again. It was very faint, way off in the distance. At first he thought his ears were playing tricks on him, or that he was dreaming. But after he pinched himself to make sure he was awake, the sound was still there. It was the sound of chanting.

"HUMONGO BONGO RONGO VINCI TEI! HUMONGO BONGO RONGO VINCI TEI!"

Bongo looked off in the direction from which he had come. There, on the horizon, was a little, squirmy column of what appeared to be ants. Of course Bongo knew that it wasn't a column of ants. It was a column of Peanut people. And they were marching onto the Purple Plain.

"Pongo! Look!"

Pongo was already looking. He had been watching the army of Peanuts for several minutes before Bongo first noticed them. "I thought they might be coming," he said. "They must have followed you. When they saw the Purple Plain, they must have thought it looked wonderful, just the way you did at first."

"And now," said Bongo sadly, "they want to be here, don't they?"

"I'm afraid so. None of us, big or small, are ever satisfied with what we have. We always think there's something better over the horizon." Pongo sighed. "It's time for us to leave, Bongo. Come along."

The two started off, walking in the opposite direction, away from the Peanut invasion.

In recent months, Bongo had moved out of the Wood into one side of the Rocky Ridge and out the other, then into one side of the Purple Plain and out the other. So, where did he end up? Right back where he started. In the Wood.

He followed Pongo into the cool shade and, now that he was home again, a warm and soothing sense of relief washed over him. He felt better than he had felt for the past year. Yes, it had been almost a year since Bongo first went for his walk. In just a few weeks he would be ninety-nine years old.

Pongo went to his old familiar place under the tallest melon tree and sat down. Bongo wasn't nearly calm enough to just sit. He jumped around and rolled on the ground. He sniffed the aromas of buddy blossom and pine that were in the air. He stuck his head right into the milkfall and took several Humongo swallows. He picked twenty-five honey melons and ate them in five big gulps, five melons to a gulp. He ate them rinds and all. Finally, feeling stuffed and exhausted, he went to his own familiar spot near the milkfall and flopped down to rest.

The two Humongos sat silently for the rest of the day. As night fell, Bongo looked up. Beyond the tree-tops, stars were out in profusion. All three moons were shining brightly.

Within two minutes he saw four meteors streak across the sky. It was marvellous to be home, but no matter how hard Bongo tried, he couldn't manage to forget the adventures he'd had. Most of all, he couldn't forget the bad feelings that had so wounded his heart.

"What if they come back?" he asked. "What if the Peanuts come back?"

"Back to the Wood? I don't think they will," Pongo replied. "They didn't really like it here. They probably won't like it on the Purple Plain either. They'll end

up back in the Rocky Ridge. They'll go on with their lives, just as we will. The old ones will die. The warriors will become the new old ones. Sooner or later they'll forget about the things that happened when they tried to explore other worlds. New ones will be born. They'll look at the Wood and think that it's a dark, mysterious place, and they'll dream about terrible monsters that might live there in the shadows. But they'll stay where they are. Not so much because they're afraid, but because that's where they feel comfortable. It's all about what you get used to, Bongo. Familiarity encourages contentment."

"What an absurd planet this is," said Bongo. "I could get used to dilly weed and puddle pudding if I tried. The Peanuts could get used to honey melons and milk. We could all . . . all of us . . . share everything!"

"That would be nice," said Pongo without much enthusiasm, "but I can't imagine it happening any time soon."

"Too bad," said Bongo with a sigh.

"Yes, truly. It is too bad."

"Oh, well. Nothing to do but wait. Wait to see what happens next."

And so they waited. And waited. And waited some more.

Then one morning, when the two were off in the Wood trying to decide which melons to pick for breakfast, they came upon a bright green object that was shaped like an elongated ball. It was very large. Its rounded top reached as high up as Bongo's knees.

"What is it, Pongo?" asked Bongo excitedly. "I've never seen anything like it before."

"Yes you have," Pongo replied. "Only you saw it from the inside."

"From the inside? When? I don't remember."

"Of course you don't. When you saw it, you hadn't hatched yet. It's an egg, Bongo. A Humongo egg. There's going to be a new baby."

"A baby!" Bongo exclaimed. "What fun! Oh, what fabulous FUN!"

Then, after thinking for a moment, Bongo said, "But . . . the egg wasn't here yesterday. How in the world did it get here?"

"I don't know," Pongo answered. "Just as I don't know how

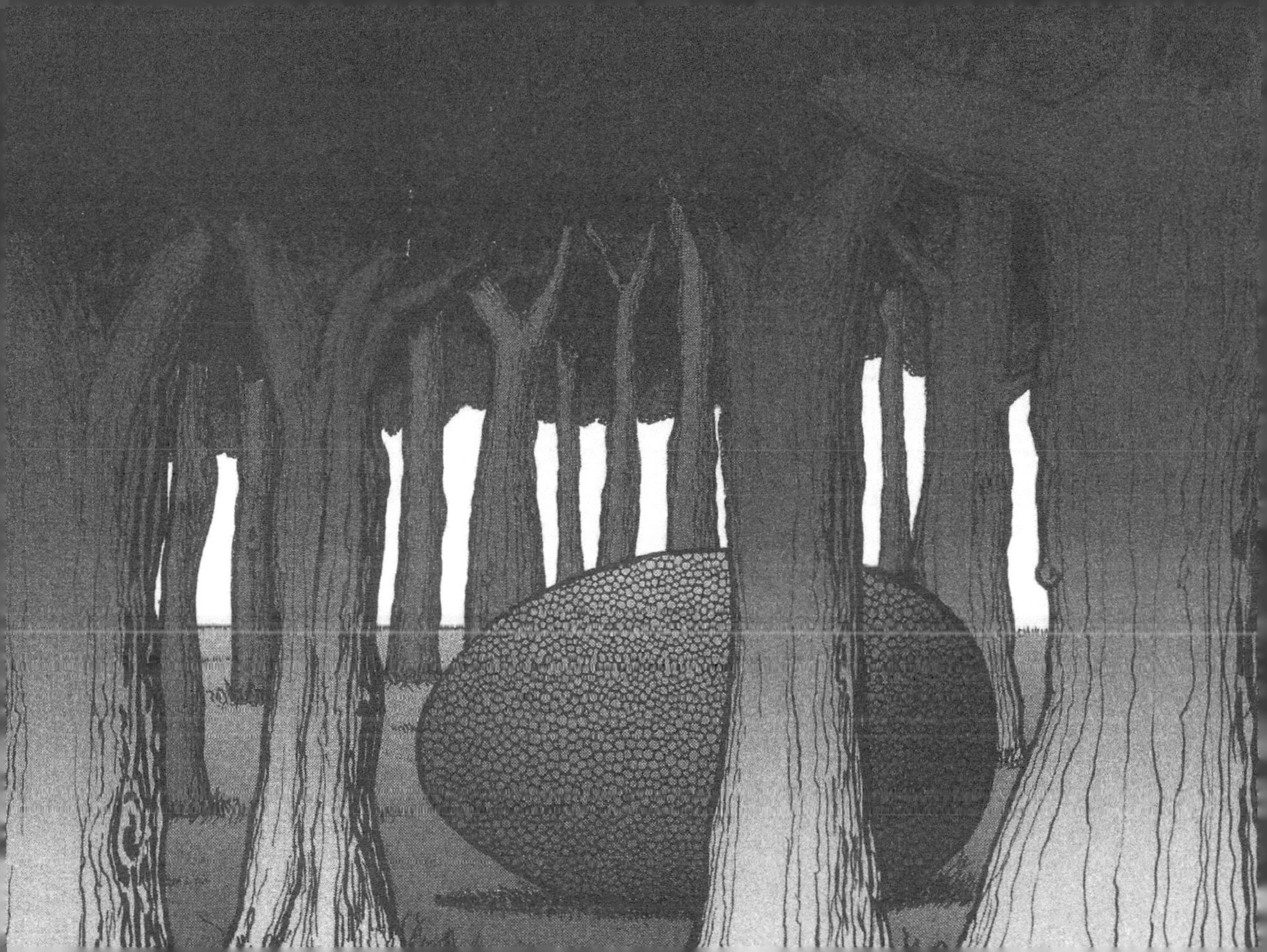

your egg got here. Or mine. I think that . . . we're not meant to understand."

That was too complicated for Bongo to think about. "A BABY!" he shouted, barely able to contain himself. "Oh, we are going to have such a good time!"

"Yes," said Pongo quietly. "A good time." He didn't seem very excited. In fact, he seemed worried.

"Pongo. Aren't you happy about the baby?"

"Yes, I'm happy, but . . . this is such a small planet. I don't know if there's going to be room. I was worried when your egg came. Now there are going to be three of us. What if there are more on the way? What if every hundred years . . . Bongo, what if another egg comes every hundred years?"

"There's plenty of room, Pongo. Plenty of room."

"If there are more of us . . . many of us . . . we'll have to move around to the other worlds to find food. The Purple Plain. The Rocky Ridge."

"Oh," said Bongo, suddenly realizing why Pongo was worried. "I see the problem. You're afraid of the Peanuts."

"I'm not afraid of the Peanuts, I'm afraid for them."

"What do you mean?"

"I'm afraid of what we Humongos might do if we were to run out of room. If we were hungry. Thirsty. Needed a place to sleep. One of us might . . ."

Bongo finished the thought for him, "One of us might destroy the Peanuts. That's what you're worried about, isn't it?"

"That, yes. But I'm more afraid of what might happen after."

"After?"

"Will we turn on each other, Bongo? Will we fight amongst ourselves because each one of us wants what the next one has?"

"You worry too much," said Bongo, dismissing the thought. "You didn't hurt the Peanuts. Neither did I. There was a moment . . . a moment when I wanted to. But I didn't do it."

"That's what frightens me, Bongo. That moment. That dangerous moment. If one of us were to do the wrong thing when that moment came . . . it could never be taken back."

"You won't do the wrong thing, Pongo. You worry too much to ever do the wrong thing. Now that I'm getting older, I seem to be worrying a lot, too, so I probably won't do the wrong thing either."

"The new one in the egg. What will he or she do? And if there are others that come after him . . . what will they do?"

"I don't know," said Bongo. "But if eggs only come every hundred years we have plenty of time to think about it."

"Yes. We'll think about it. We'll think about it while we wait for the next thing to happen. Just as I've said all along, Bongo. All we can do is wait."

"I never thought I'd say this, but you're right. All we can do is wait."

They waited for two weeks. Bongo's birthday came along. As a special surprise, Pongo gave him two pine-butter-cones that he'd buried a few winters back. It was a treat for Bongo to taste a pine-butter-cone in the summertime. He gave the second one back to Pongo so that he could have a treat too. Bongo believed in sharing. If only he could make the Peanuts understand that it made him happy to share.

Then one morning, the giant green egg began to make little scratching noises. That is, whatever . . . whoever . . . was inside the egg began to make little scratching noises. The egg couldn't make little scratching noises on its own.

Bongo had known from the day they had found the egg that there was a baby coming, but it had never seemed quite real to him, not until that morning. When he heard those little noises, he suddenly appreciated the fact that there was something alive inside that shell and that it was getting ready to hatch.

"Pongo," he asked, "what if the baby doesn't want to just sit here and wait? What if he wants to walk to the edge of the Wood?"

"I'm sure he will. But not until he's nearly a hundred. It takes a hundred years or so for a soul to become restless."

"After a hundred years . . . maybe things will be different. Maybe the new Humongo won't ever get restless."

"Maybe. We'll have to wait and see."

They waited for a few more days.

The next thing that happened was . . .

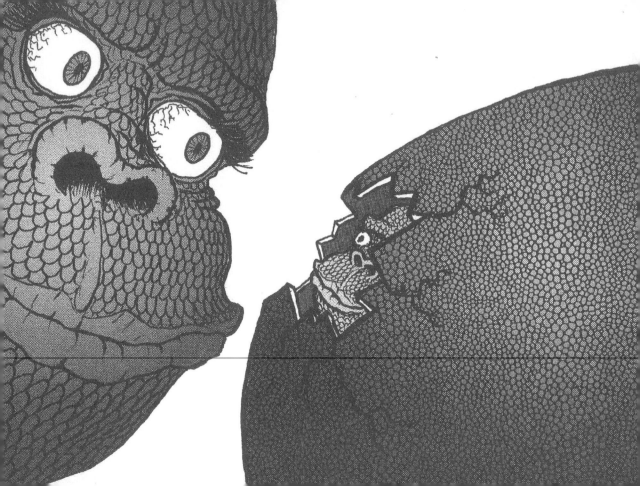

... the egg hatched.

TO BE CONTINUED

(Now we all just have to wait!)

ABOUT THE AUTHOR

George Andrew Romero was an American-Canadian filmmaker and editor, best known for his series of gruesome and satirical horror films about an imagined zombie apocalypse, beginning with *Night of the Living Dead*.

He died on July 16, 2017.

GEORGE A. ROMERO ON *THE LITTLE WORLD OF HUMONGO BONGO*
INTERVIEW BY DAVE ALEXANDER

DA: Let's begin with your early years. What were some of your favourite books as a child?

GAR: I used to read these books about Don Camillo, a priest in Spain. They were for younger readers, and one of them was called *The Little World of Don Camillo*. The title of [*Humongo Bongo*] is from that. They were all little adventures, and actually, there's a film version that was made for that one [in 1952]. They were all just little adventures around this village.

DA: What books did you read to your own children?

GAR: The regular ones: *There's a Mouse About the House!* and *Goodnight Moon*. All the usual suspects.

DA: *How did* The Little World of Humongo Bongo *come about?*
GAR: There was a Belgian publisher that wanted to do a project where they asked improbable film people to write for young readers, and I'm one of the guys they asked. I don't know who else they asked. Honestly, it just sort of blew by quickly. And it was only published in French, in Belgium.

DA: *Given that this was such a departure from the work you'd been doing up to that point, what was your reaction when they approached you about the project?*
GAR: That's why I decided to do it. I thought, "Wow, this might be neat." I wanted to do a little parable with a social conscience. So I just jumped on it.

DA: *How did you become the illustrator as well?*
GAR: I'm not a wonderful artist but they had heard that I'd

studied art so they asked if I wanted to illustrate it too. I studied painting and design when I was in college. I was always doing movie posters—just basically copying them, I didn't do any originals. I was copying *Ben-Hur* and *The Ten Commandments* and other movies that were out at the time.

DA: *What were some of the things that influenced* Humongo Bongo?
GAR: I used to do this little comic book character—it never went anywhere, I never published it or anything—which was called "A Caveman Called Gorok." The way Humongo looks is sort of modelled after that. It's a little more reptilian but the face is modelled after that character that I used to draw.

DA: *Who, or what, is Humongo Bongo?*
GAR: [Chuckles] I don't care. He's just an unfortunate being that happened to turn up in the wrong place at the wrong time.

DA: Do you relate to the character in any specific way?
GAR: No, I was just trying to tell a little parable about overpopulation, tolerance, intolerance, and a whole bunch of other little themes that were thrown in there. I was just hoping for young readers to think about it. I think there's almost no wrong way to think about it. It's just circumstances, the way they are.

DA: How did you approach the illustrations?
GAR: I did them on posterboards. I just did them for this project; they never went anywhere else. I used pen and ink, and then I used these zipatones for some of the textures. They were these things you could buy at an art supply store; you would lay them over and press it on, and it gives you a pattern, like a tile pattern or scale pattern. All of the little patterns in there? I didn't draw those so meticulously; they were all zipatone patterns.

DA: *How long did it take to finish the book?*
GAR: Three months, with the drawings.

DA: *Would you consider it an enjoyable experience?*
GAR: I enjoyed it a lot. It was like taking a breather, getting away from the everyday.

DA: *Did it make you want to do another kids book?*
GAR: I wouldn't say no. [laughs] I have very often, particularly now, thought about it. I would welcome the opportunity to do something more. I've thought that I should have a branch-off career. I get sick and tired of trying to promote films. It gets old. You know, you never earn your platinum card. Every time you have to go through the grind again and sell people on who you are. It's just pretty tiring, so I have been wanting to just write.

DA: Any specific idea for other books?
GAR: None that I'm really prepared to talk about. I have a lot of ideas spinning but nothing that's ready to discuss.

DA: How does it feel to have it republished, over two decades later?
GAR: I'd always hoped for it. The original publisher tried to get an English publisher interested but they couldn't find anybody. So I'm delighted. The only copies I have are in French and I can't read 'em!

DA: What do you think kids should take away from this story?
GAR: The theme of intolerance is the thing that really stands out the most to me, and is the most pertinent today—people not being able to come to terms with other kinds of people. That's the theme that will stand out the most.

DA: Did you always envision the story as something that an adult audience could key into, as well, in terms of the subtext?

GAR: I was hoping that it would cross the line. I have actually gotten some responses from adult readers who liked it. They respond to the whole idea of overpopulation, and the intolerance. The themes that are in there, I think they're pretty obvious as big, overriding themes.

DA: Do you feel that those themes resonate more today than when the book was published?

GAR: I think maybe the intolerance theme does, particularly in the Trump era.

DA: Is it a pessimistic, realistic, or optimistic view of human nature?
GAR: I'm afraid it's probably pessimistic. The main characters keep on keepin' on, so there's hope. I may want to carry that on if I ever do another, but we'll see. . . .

———◆✕◆———

UNTOLD HORROR is a brand dedicated to exploring and—when possible—resurrecting genre stories that never got off the ground for one reason or another. Anchored by—as of this writing—an in-development documentary series that will tell the stories behind the stories, it chiefly focuses on films that died in Development Hell, or were transformed into something radically different than the original creator intended. But occasionally other rarities are revealed, such as the book you're holding.

Created by Toronto-based Dave Alexander (former editor-in-chief of *Rue Morgue* magazine) and Ottawa screenwriter Mark Pollesel in 2016, Untold Horror is designed as a multi-platform monster for fans, by fans. Because if there's one thing writers like Stephen King have taught us time and time again . . . sometimes, they come back. . . .

Find us at UNTOLDHORROR.CA